STRIVING TOGETHER

A statement of th
governed the ai
Evangelical M

J. ELWYN DAVIES

EVANGELICAL PRESS OF WALES

First published 1984
ISBN 0 900898 83 6

Cover design by
Rhiain M. Davies

Published by the Evangelical Press of Wales,
Bryntirion, Bridgend, Mid Glamorgan CF31 4DX
Printed by the Talbot Printing Co. Ltd.,
Port Talbot, West Glamorgan

Contents

'that ye stand fast in
one spirit, with one mind
striving together for the
faith of the gospel'

(Philippians 1 : 27)

1
In retrospect

THE Evangelical Movement of Wales first appeared on the Welsh church scene as a result of steps which evangelical ministers and others felt obliged to take in the years immediately after the Second World War. They were motivated by a concern for evangelism, but also for the spiritual well-being of those who shared their convictions but who found themselves placed at considerable disadvantage in churches and denominations which, to a very considerable extent, had departed from the main tenets of the Christian faith. The hope at the time was that if such believers could be strengthened to witness faithfully to their Lord and Saviour, others would be added to their number, and in this way ground which had been lost for decades would be regained.

In 1948, at the end of what had been a remarkable week of evangelism at Bala in North Wales, a Welsh-language bimonthly magazine was launched (*Y Cylchgrawn Efengylaidd*). This was followed in 1952 by an invitation to its readers, many of whom were by now being encouraged to meet regularly in 'evangelical fellowships' or *seiadau*, to attend the first Welsh-language annual conference. In the summer of 1954, the first 'camp' for young people was held at

Bangor, North Wales, to be followed a few years later by a full bilingual programme of camps extending throughout the summer holidays. The first issue of *The Evangelical Magazine of Wales,* the English counterpart to the Welsh magazine, appeared in the summer of 1954, and this in turn led to the convening of the first English annual conference at Sandfields, Aberafan, in August 1956. The following year saw the emergence of the first ministers' conference to be convened under the auspices of 'The Evangelical Movement of Wales' (the title adopted in 1955—see p.45), and this led to the formation that same year of a network of ministers' fellowships meeting throughout the land and pursuing a common course of study.

In those early years, there was no thought of inviting churches to be officially associated with the work, for the good and sufficient reason that the churches where such people were to be found would have resisted any form of identification with an avowedly evangelical fraternity. The few truly evangelical churches that were in being either belonged to an existing denomination or, by way of reaction to denominationalism generally, would have been wary of entering into any form of association with a wider fellowship.

In 1967, however, it was decided to make it possible for churches to be associated with the Movement. What prompted this step and made it inevitable were the same considerations as had guided the work from its inception—concern for the truth of God and for the well-being of His people. The *historical* factors which brought about such an important development need, however, to be recounted in some detail.

In the mid-sixties, an event took place which highlighted the extent to which the churches of Wales had departed from their own historical standards and from the great body of truth revealed in Holy Scripture. The late Sir David James offered a considerable sum of money to the major nonconformist denominations, provided that they could achieve unity within a given period. This well-intentioned, if misguided, gesture proved to be a veritable shot in the arm for the ecumenical movement in Wales at the time. The offer was taken up with considerable enthusiasm.

In the course of the next few years, proposals for church union were prepared which made it quite obvious to those of an evangelical persuasion that no attempt was going to be made to offer scriptural justification for the new church structures that were envisaged. It became equally evident that whatever church structure were eventually recommended, its doctrinal standards would have to be broad enough to accommodate individuals and churches of widely divergent views. As a result, those who still believed in the central truths of the orthodox Christian faith, however reluctant they might have been before to acknowledge the extent and gravity of the doctrinal landslide that had taken place in the churches, were suddenly made to see involvement in those churches in a very different light.

Prior to this, it was possible for evangelical Christians to argue that it was their intention to work together to bring their churches back to the foundational truths that had long since been abandoned. They now realized, however, that they belonged to churches and denominations whose leaders were quite prepared to see their own fellowships absorbed into a new church structure where truths precious to evangelical believers would be relegated to the status of a not very convincing 'interpretation' adhered to by a few old-fashioned obscurantists. Such people, of course, would be accommodated in the united church—indeed they would be welcomed—but on the tacit understanding that they acknowledged their view of the gospel to be merely an interpretation, to be placed alongside other interpretations equally valid if not more so.

At this time, those who were responsible for the leadership of the EMW, together with the ministers who attended the ministers' fellowships, decided to apply themselves with a measure of urgency to the study of the doctrine of the church.

They wanted to ascertain for themselves how churches conforming to the pattern of the New Testament should be ordered, in what way they should be related to each other, what their doctrinal standards should be, who would qualify for membership, how the sacraments were to be administered, etc.[1] It was generally assumed at the time that they had to be prepared for the day when their churches and denominations would be absorbed into a new ecclesiastical structure—a structure which, in every probability, would be further removed from New Testament standards than anything they had known hitherto.

Something else took place at that time—a development which was to prove of even greater consequence. When these matters were being considered, evangelicals who were endeavouring to respond to their serious implications were suddenly confronted with a yet more sobering challenge. As a consequence, the process of reformation which had begun when they had been forced to ask very basic questions concerning the nature of the church and its ordinances was given a completely new impetus, and that from a not altogether unexpected quarter. Failure to mention this would render us guilty of doing gross injustice to the way in which, under God, we were brought to our present persuasion. It would also lay us open to the charge of having been nothing better than crass scaremongers, responding to an event which never happened. For, as is commonly accepted, the proposals advocated in the 'Scheme of Union', as it was called, are as far from fulfilment today as they have ever been.

The late Dr. D. M. Lloyd-Jones had been persuaded for some time that the doctrine of the church had long been neglected by evangelicals. As part of his understanding of the New Testament teaching on the nature of the church, he now argued that the only people who could be guilty of the sin of schism were those who in reality belonged to the body of

[1] Eventually the fruit of these studies was published in two booklets, *The Christian Church—a Biblical Study* (EMW 1966) and *The Ministry and Life of the Christian Church* (EMW 1968).

Christ. And his challenge to evangelicals was plain and direct. If, according to their understanding of the New Testament doctrine of the church, only those who had known the 'washing of regeneration and the sanctification of the Spirit' were in the body of Christ, then those who maintained that they were in that category, and yet remained separated from one another in different denominations, were guilty of the sin of schism. They (and they alone) could be guilty of that sin. Furthermore, by remaining in the historic denominations they were recognizing the ministry of men who denied their Lord. In other words, serious wrong was being committed against the Lord Jesus Christ Himself and against His church—the institution which the Lord had ordained for the good of His people. It was therefore the duty of all who were concerned to do His will to ask themselves two basic and fundamental questions: 'What is a Christian?' and 'What is a church?'

As a result of the deliberations that followed, gradually but inevitably, new churches committed to the evangelical faith began to appear in different parts of Wales. In order to discuss matters of mutual concern, their leaders began to meet in 'Church Issues Conferences' sponsored by the Movement.[1] The question had already been taken up of providing theological training for those who, for reasons of conscience as well as circumstance, would not be able to attend theological colleges associated with the historic denominations.[2]

It was in anticipation of such a time as this, when new churches would begin to enquire with what wider fellowship of churches they ought to be associated, that the General Committee of the Movement felt it right, first, to settle as a matter of principle how churches ought to be related to each

[1] The first of these was held in January 1974.

[2] The four-year Theological Training Course launched in August 1972 consists of three parts: two residential weeks per annum; a prescribed course of study throughout the year; and, wherever possible, help and instruction from a local pastor. A parallel Welsh-language Course was commenced in 1982.

other, and, then, to commend such a provision to the people of God in our day. It would need to be a provision indigenous to God's people in both the Welsh- and English-speaking parts of our land, and faithful to the rich spiritual heritage of our forefathers. Above all, it would have to be a provision regulated by and consistent with the teachings of the Word of God. For we totally reject the view, favoured by those who wish to justify long-inherited ecclesiastical indiscretions, that the Scriptures offer inadequate guidance with respect to the way churches are to order their lives. The Scriptures are sufficient for *all* matters of faith and conduct. Indeed it would be difficult to think of any doctrine whose implications could have a greater bearing on the preservation and propagation of the faith, and the conduct which it demands of us, than the doctrine of the church—the way God's people are to relate to one another and to learn to respect those who are charged with responsibility for their spiritual well-being. 'The church of the living God', according to the apostle Paul, is 'the pillar and ground of the truth' (1 Tim. 3:15). Knowing how we ought to 'behave [ourselves] in the house of God' is therefore a matter of the greatest consequence.

The question which the leaders of the EMW had to ask, and which every church of the Lord Jesus Christ faithful to His precepts and teachings has to face, is a very important one. Should churches be associated in any way with a wider fellowship? Is it not sufficient for them to fend for themselves, provided that they are prepared to respond to requests for help arising spontaneously from other Christians and from other Christian churches? Was this not the pattern of New Testament church life? Indeed, is there not a danger that any wider expression of fellowship, however loosely and honourably conceived, will eventually encroach upon the domain of the local church, threaten its autonomy, and even at times, by virtue of the very fact of association, involve it in uncalled-for embarrassment? Furthermore, does not history teach us that any form of 'association' between churches *introduces* a schismatic element? Inevitably distinctions will be drawn between churches which 'belong' and those which do not. What value, then, our avowed concern for evangelical unity?

The answer which as a Movement we have been obliged to give to all these questions has been influenced by the following scriptural consideration:

The Head of the church has imposed upon His followers in this world obligations which go beyond our obligations to one another within the context of our local church fellowship. In order to honour those obligations some means of identification is called for, together with a modicum of organization for the provision of necessary services. These are not to be provided, however, in such a way as will divide the Lord's people, but rather in such a spirit and manner as will increasingly unite them in the truth and in the pursuit of all that is required of them as children of God here on earth.

To these considerations and their practical outworking in our day we now turn.

2
The Body of Christ

With Christians of all ages, we believe that a local church is given visible and tangible expression *when a community of believers covenant to worship and to serve God together in accordance with the teachings of His Word and the leading of the Holy Spirit.* Notwithstanding the possibility—indeed the probability—that there will be a small element whose faith is purely nominal, such a fellowship constitutes a valid expression of the body of Christ in any day or age.

We make this our starting-point. To belong to the body of Christ, one has first to belong to Christ. It is such people, and only such, who constitute the body of Christ. In other words, we totally reject the concept of a historic 'church' which, regardless of what it teaches (e.g. on salvation and conditions of membership), maintains that it—and in the case of the Roman Catholic Church, in the past at least, it alone—represents the body of Christ. 'Now ye are the body of Christ, and members in particular', says the Apostle, writing to 'the church of God which is at Corinth, *to them that are sanctified in Christ Jesus, called to be saints'* (1 Cor. 12:27; 1:2).

As Christians, however, we also believe that we belong to a wider community of believers, who worship and serve God in many 'local' churches—those to whom the Apostle refers in the concluding part of his salutation to the church at Corinth: *'with all that in every place call upon the name of Jesus Christ our Lord, both theirs and ours'.* It is our conviction that all such Christians and Christian churches, taken together, constitute an equally valid expression of the body of Christ in any day or age. 'There is one body', says the Apostle, writing to the church at Ephesus, and 'we are members of his body, of his flesh, and of his bones' (Eph. 4:4; 5:30). In that description he evidently has in mind, in the *first* instance, all the children of God living at the time and functioning as interrelated members of a human body. In a related but subordinate sense he includes by inference all who have gone before as well as those who have yet to be added to the body: 'Till we all come into the unity of the faith' etc. (Eph. 4:13). But the *predominant* emphasis is upon the body as it functions in the living present, in this world.

In other words, while we believe that each community of believers worshipping together in a given locality *is* the church, the body of Christ, we also believe that such churches are not to be thought of in isolation from other churches. Taken together, too, they constitute the body of Christ. 'So we, being many,' says the Apostle to the church at Rome, 'are one body in Christ, and every one members one of another' (Rom. 12:5). That is why, in New Testament days, Christians who worshipped in local congregations were acutely aware of the fact that they belonged to a wider community of believers, from whom, from time to time, they would receive messages, ministerial visits, or even appeals for financial help.

Indeed, we would go further. According to the clear teaching of the Word of God and the example of the early church, not only do we as Christians belong to the one body of Christ, in the sense of the wider community of believers, but we also have *obligations* to that body. These obligations are additional and complementary to the primary obligations we have towards one another within the fellowship of the local church where God has placed us. They must not override the latter, but neither must they be disregarded. Indeed, it would be our contention that the *means* which God has ordained for giving expression to the unity we have as Christians is *the honouring of the mutual obligations which He has laid upon us*—e.g. to love one another (John 13:34,35) and to pursue that oneness of mind, heart and life which will be the outcome of our being 'sanctified in the truth' (John 17:17-23). It is the honouring of these obligations that is to tell the world that we are one, not the provision of a self-perpetuating hierarchy of priests and bishops headed by a Pope, speciously claiming that it constitutes 'the visible sign (and source) of the unity of the whole Church'. Today, as in the past, such hierarchical superstructures, whether Catholic or Protestant, have only served to perpetuate 'churches' which have long since departed from New Testament doctrines and standards.

To those obligations we therefore turn. We do so believing that the EMW (however inadequately) represents a sincere effort in our own day to honour these obligations and to meet them. Indeed we would do well to explain at this point that *it is because of our conviction that these obligations form part of the mutual responsibility of all Christians, and of all churches faithful to the Word of God, that churches are invited to affiliate with the EMW*.

They may be summarized as follows:

1. As Christians we are under a solemn obligation to bear witness to the world that we are one (John 17:21,23; Eph. 4:3; 1 Peter 2:9).
2. In a world where the Antichrist is as active today as he has ever been, we are also under a solemn obligation to dissociate ourselves from all those who, though avowedly Christian, deny our Lord (Matt. 7:15-23; Gal. 1:9; 1 John 4:1-6; 2 John 10,11).
3. If we are to heed the desires and intentions of our Lord and Saviour Jesus Christ, we are under a further obligation to endeavour always to bring as many as

possible of God's children into that unity in the truth—that oneness of belief, life and conduct—for which our Lord prayed (John 17:17-23; Eph. 4:11-13).

4. We need to acknowledge that the Head of the church would have certain functions and services performed which are for the mutual benefit of all the churches (Eph. 4:11-13).

In the following chapters we shall consider each obligation in turn.

3
We are one

It would be our submission that as Christians, and as members of Christian churches, *we are under a solemn obligation to tell the world that we are one.* Unfortunately we cannot tell the world that we are one on *all* matters, nor that, as yet, we are one in the sense that our Lord had in mind when He prayed His high-priestly prayer, '*As* thou, Father, art in me, and I in thee, that they also may be one in us.' That, as we shall explain later, is an objective to be sought, an ideal to be realized (see pp.26-35). Nevertheless, by virtue of the miracle of regeneration and the anointing which we have received from 'the Holy One' (1 John 2:20,27), we find that we have already embraced a considerable body of truth which would otherwise be completely unacceptable to us.

With respect to *those* truths we are one—not that anyone would suggest that we all understand their implications with equal clarity, or indeed that any of us will understand them fully in this life—eternity will be 'too short to utter all His praise'. Nevertheless, to quote the apostle John, 'The truth' abides in 'all those who have known the truth', and 'shall be with us for ever' (2 John 1,2). 'His seed remaineth' in us, and as a consequence we cannot any more sin heedlessly (1 John

3:9).[1] 'I have not written unto you because ye know not the truth, but because ye know it, and that no lie is of the truth' (1 John 2:21). This is why the apostle Paul insists that Christians *now* enjoy a unity of the Spirit which only needs to be *kept* in the bond of peace (Eph. 4:3).

We acknowledge that our Lord is not satisfied with a unity that is less than a unity in all the truth. That is why He prayed, 'Sanctify them *through thy truth* . . . that they all may be one; as thou, Father, art in me, and I in thee, that they also may be one in us' (John 17:17,21). That is also why, through the ages, the ascended Lord has given gifts of ministry to His people, that all may come 'into the unity of the faith, and of the knowledge of the Son of God, unto a perfect man, unto the measure of the stature of the fulness of Christ' (Eph. 4:13). But as we know that one consequence of the unity which our Lord wants to achieve is 'that the world may know that thou hast sent me, and hast loved them, as thou hast loved me' (John 17:23), it is our duty and responsibility, as far as we are able, to give expression to that unity, even though it is not complete or perfected as yet. And one way in which we can do this is patently obvious. Rather than placarding to the world at what point(s) we differ from our brethren, as has been the custom of evangelical Christians in the past, we should be telling the world that with respect to very many truths we are one. Nothing would be more likely to persuade men that our Lord is the Son of God, and that we are the loved ones of God, than a solemn declaration of common allegiance to those truths by means of which God has separated us from the world and sanctified us to Himself. This in and of itself is not enough, as we shall see later, but it is surely where we need to begin.

Indeed, we would go further. It is through the declaration of those truths, whether it be in the form of a confession of

[1] The apostle Peter tells us what constitutes 'God's seed'—'Being born again, not of corruptible seed, but of incorruptible, by the word of God . . . And this is the word which by the gospel is preached unto you' (1 Peter 1:23,25).

faith, written testimony, or the spoken or preached word, that God has decreed that the eyes of the blind shall be opened. If there are other overriding considerations which, in our judgment, necessitate our telling the world where we differ from our brethren, this should surely place us under an *even greater obligation* to tell the world that with respect to a great many truths, and their glorious outworking in our lives, we are one.

That is why we believe that evangelical churches in our land should be prepared to make it known publicly, in whatever way is best suited to their particular circumstances, that with respect to *these* truths they are at one with their brethren. The Movement's Doctrinal Belief offers such a statement of truth (see Appendix A). And the first reason we give for having made provision for churches to be affiliated with the Movement is that by such identification churches are enabled to inform the world of the extent to which they are at one with all their brethren. This does *not* mean that we regard those matters upon which they may differ from their brethren as unimportant. Nor does it mean that it would be our wish or intention that such differences be ignored or swept under the carpet (see chapter 5). It simply means that we begin at this point. We recognize that we are under a scriptural obligation to tell the world that we belong to the one family of God, and that there is a very considerable body of truth to which we owe our salvation and count it our privilege to bear common testimony.

This is why, as a first condition of affiliation with the Movement, churches are required to declare their agreement with the Movement's Doctrinal Belief (see Appendix B). In our judgment, this doctrinal standard represents the very considerable body of truths which every true believer is able to confess. Christians may differ in their view of other truths: upon these cardinal truths there would be agreement.

It is our desire, therefore, that all churches whose doctrinal standards embrace these truths should identify themselves with each other in terms of this basis. Such churches in their own doctrinal standards are free to *add* other statements of truth upon which they and their officers are agreed, on condition that such additions in no way contradict or are inconsistent with the basic tenets of the Movement's Doctrinal Belief. They may add, but they may not subtract. That is why we state in our Constitution: 'each congregation [affiliated to the Movement] shall determine its own form of government and ministry in the light of its understanding of the New Testament'; and also, 'each congregation shall determine its own mode of baptism and its significance in relation to the membership of the local church', provided it is agreed that 'its observance never automatically conveys regenerative grace' and that 'its subjects shall be, as far as it is possible to ascertain, believers (in the case of believers' baptism) and the children of believers (in the case of infant baptism)'. (See Appendix B.)

In this way, by allowing for such variations of doctrinal position as are not inconsistent with our commitment to the great corpus of truth commonly believed among us (whilst at the same time insisting upon allegiance to these truths which are common to all), we avoid becoming a denomination, where one 'denominator' (e.g. our view of baptism, church government, the order of salvation, the doctrine of the Spirit or eschatology) is allowed to have more of an influence upon our relationships with other Christians within the body of Christ than the fact that we are in that body at all and hold so many doctrines in common.

4
We differ

There is another reason why churches that uphold the evangelical faith are under an obligation to declare to the world the doctrines upon which they are united. There are many churches in our land today which, regrettably, have no right to the title 'evangelical' or even 'Christian', the gospel preached in their pulpits and believed by their members being nothing less than a perversion of the gospel of the Lord Jesus Christ. *Evangelical churches are therefore under a solemn obligation to make it abundantly clear to the world that they differ from such churches.* Without a public intimation of distinctiveness and difference, how will the world come to know and to believe, through *our* oneness in Him, that Jesus Christ is the Son of God and that Christians are those upon whom God has set His love from eternity?

Those whom the Father has 'given' to the Son, who have come to believe upon Him through the word and testimony of the apostles, *must* be distinguished from those who maintain that they are equally Christian *but who deny that testimony*, feeling that they have no need to come to the Saviour or that the Saviour should come to them 'that they might have life'. It is the oneness of the former over against the latter that will convince the world that the Lord Jesus Christ is the Sent One of God, and that we have been loved by God from all eternity: 'That *they* all may be one; as thou, Father, art in me, and I in thee, that *they* also may be one in us: that the world may believe that thou hast sent me' (John 17:21).

The Apostle's injunction to the churches of Galatia is no less relevant or urgent today:

> 'If any man preach any other gospel unto you than that ye have received, let him be accursed' (Gal. 1:9).

Or the words of the apostle John:

> 'Beloved, believe not every spirit, but try the spirits whether they are of God: because many false prophets are gone out into the world. Hereby know ye the Spirit of God: every spirit that confesseth that Jesus Christ is come in the flesh is of God: and every spirit that confesseth not that Jesus Christ is come in the flesh is not of God: and this is that spirit of antichrist, whereof ye have heard that it should come; and even now already is it in the world' (1 John 4:1-3).

Or again:

> 'If there come any unto you, and bring not this doctrine, receive him not into your house, neither bid him God speed: for he that biddeth him God speed is partaker of his evil deeds' (2 John 10,11).

And finally the words of our Lord:

> 'Beware of false prophets, which come to you in sheep's clothing, but inwardly they are ravening wolves. Ye shall know them by their fruits . . . Not every one that saith unto me, Lord, Lord, shall enter into the kingdom of heaven; but he that doeth the will of my Father which is in heaven' (Matt. 7:15,16,21).

In the genial, and yet doctrinally lethal, 'ecumenical' atmosphere that prevails today, those who dare even to suggest that such sentiments are to be taken seriously will immediately be accused of the twin ecclesiastical sins of our day—arrogance and uncharitableness. With such, however, we have to take our stand and ask two questions, not in any spirit of pride, but from hearts which, by the grace of God, may claim to 'know the truth' (John 3:11; 1 John 2:20,21,27; 2 John 1,2). We ask, Who is being arrogant? Might it not be those who arrogate to themselves the right to contradict, edit or amend what the Lord Jesus Christ said concerning Himself and the Father whose Person and will He came to reveal? Secondly, Who is being uncharitable? Is it an act of charity to tamper with or to flinch from proclaiming the message our Lord came to deliver (unpalatable as it undoubtedly is to fallen human nature), when the glory of God and man's eternal destiny are at stake?

This is why all officers, committee members, speakers of the Movement itself, its fellowships and affiliated churches are required to subscribe to the Movement's statement of doctrinal belief (see Appendix A, sections (a) and (b)).

It is for this reason also that churches affiliated with the Movement are described in our Constitution as consisting of *'those, and only those, who, professing faith in Jesus Christ, the eternal Son of God, as Saviour, Lord and God, whose death in their place constitutes the only ground of their salvation, have forsaken their sin and now seek to live a life of holiness by the power of the Holy Spirit'.* Churches which in practice hold to a view of the Christian church which is different from this are debarred from the fellowship and testimony that is represented by the Evangelical Movement of Wales.

This does not mean that we deny the possibility that there may be regenerate believers in such churches, or that those who preach in their pulpits, whether regularly or intermittently, may be true preachers of the gospel. We speak of *churches,* and it is our contention that the churches of the Lord Jesus Christ, as they are portrayed in the New Testament, always consist of a predominance of truly regenerate believers. The only concession to disbelief in the New Testament is the acceptance of the inevitable presence of those who, far from being blatant deniers of the truth, imitate true believers but are in fact counterfeit believers (Matt. 13:24-30). Deniers of the truth, or false prophets as they are called in the New Testament, are always exposed and resisted. The tares, when their true identity is known, are to be tolerated. But the New Testament knows of no churches where the tares outnumber the wheat. The churches of the New Testament, by definition, consist of people whom God has called out of the world and separated unto Himself (Matt. 16:17,18). The enemy admittedly hides others among God's people, but even he takes very good care to disguise their true identity.

That is why, as a condition of affiliation with the EMW, churches are required 'to examine with charity all candidates for membership, so as to ensure, as far as humanly possible, that such persons have in fact experienced the new birth, which alone will enable them to make the above profession sincerely' (see Appendix B).

This is also why evangelical churches who are associated with an ecumenical council of churches, whose doctrinal standards—to quote again from our Constitution—'are sufficiently comprehensive to allow within its fellowship those who believe doctrines which conflict with or in any way contradict the plain meaning' of the Movement's doctrinal statement, are required to terminate that association as a condition of affiliation.

We would not insist, however, that evangelical churches which are associated with a historical church body which is guilty of doctrinal laxity should sever their links with such a body as a condition of fellowship. The issue of when to secede from a church body or denomination once loyal to the evangelical faith, but now having ceased to exercise discipline in allegiance to that faith, is left to the conscience of evangelical churches and their leadership. The fact that they have not dissociated at a given point in time is not considered sufficient reason for withholding the right to affiliate. In seeking affiliation, however, such churches are required to give a solemn undertaking that they will 'work towards the reformation of the church according to biblical principles' and give an assurance that it is their intention 'in principle and practice to work towards a scriptural expression of church unity' (see Appendix B, section (b)i,ii).

For a church to be associated *by virtue of its denominational alignment* with a council of churches or with *any* ecumenical organization that advocates the view that the Christian church can be so comprehensive in its doctrinal standards as to include within its ranks (and even in its pulpit) those who hold views which contradict and deny the truths stated in the Movement's Doctrinal Belief, would, however, be considered sufficient grounds for debarring any such church from fellowship with the Evangelical Movement of Wales. Churches desiring affiliation, and connected with a church body thus associated, are therefore required as a condition of affiliation to have officially declared their dissent from their denomination's involvement in such activities (see Appendix B, section (b)iii).

So the first two reasons we give for making provision for evangelical churches to affiliate with the Movement are that, by so doing, (i) they declare to the world that they belong to a fraternity which together owns allegiance to the evangelical faith, and (ii) they do so in contradistinction to other churches which no longer adhere to that faith. Whether all evangelical churches are affiliated to the Movement at any given point in time is beside the point. The avowed aim and intent of the fellowship is that it should be as wide as the entire complement of such churches will allow, to the exclusion of all other churches.

For some, however, such a prospect immediately poses the problem of avowedly evangelical churches being identified with similarly 'evangelical' churches with whom they would be at variance upon important matters of doctrine and, inevitably, upon the outworking of the practical implications of such doctrines. Why should any church risk the embarrassment that could be theirs as a consequence of such identification? Would it not be better to remain severely independent, or to settle for the age-long recipe of a more limited fellowship of churches which would be of one mind concerning such doctrines?

To that problem we now turn. It would be our contention that such considerations present evangelical churches with a serious and costly challenge—a challenge which needs to be faced with all the grace, resolution and wisdom that God will grant. It calls for vision. It also calls for a whole-hearted commitment to *all* the disciplines that the Head of the church has imposed upon His children while they continue here below.

5
We seek unity in the truth

Not only are Christians, and Christian churches generally, under an obligation to tell the world that they are one with respect to a very considerable body of truth; *they are also under an obligation to work together in order to help each other achieve that oneness of belief, life and conduct for which our Lord prayed in John 17.* This is the New Testament perspective, and it must be ours also.

Many Christians assume that what our Lord prayed for in the high-priestly prayer was that the apostles and those who would come to believe on Him through their word would be one. If that were the case, we would have to conclude that, despite our Lord's claim that the Father heard Him always (John 11:42), on this occasion He failed to do so. For the story of the Christian church throughout its history has been 'by schisms rent asunder'. We need not be alarmed, however. Our Lord's prayer was far more realistic and robust. Indeed, inasmuch as the Father is still responding positively to that prayer, we ought to ponder its import well, for we have a part to play in the answering of it.

What our Lord prayed on behalf of those who would believe on Him throughout the ages was not simply that they should be one, but that they should be sanctified 'through thy truth . . . that they all may be one' (John 17:17,21). That was His prayer.

Having already asked that they should be preserved from the twin perils of being lost (v.11) or of falling prey to evil or the evil one (v.15), He prayed positively that God Himself should cause them to be consecrated more and more to Himself through a proper understanding of His Word, in order that they might know a oneness of belief, life and conduct which would convince the world, firstly, that He was the Son of God (vv.21,23) and, secondly, that they themselves were the people upon whom He had set His love (v.23).

Our Lord left those who heard Him pray in no doubt as to the nature and scope of that oneness which was to characterize God's people. 'As thou, Father, art in me, and I in thee, that they also may be one in us.' *The oneness that prevails between the Father and the Son is to be the standard of the oneness in conviction, life and character which increasingly is to mark the people of God in this world*—'that they may be one, even as we are one' (v.22).

There were two factors that accounted for the oneness that characterized our Lord's relationship with the Father. In the first place, Father and Son knew that glorious inter-relationship of persons to which our Lord referred when asked by Philip to justify His claim of identification with the Father. 'Believest thou not that I am *in* the Father, and the Father *in* me?' (John 14:10; cf. 10:38). But, as our Lord went on to explain, there was a second element integral to that total identification of mind, will and purpose which existed between Father and Son, and this was that He was utterly submitted to the Father. 'The words that I speak unto you I speak not of myself: but the Father that dwelleth in me, he doeth the works.' Words and works—His entire ministry—were the works of the Father. This was why He was able to go on to say, 'He that hath seen me hath seen the Father', and on a previous occasion, 'I and my Father are one' (John 14:9; 10:30).

The first of these two elements has already been realized in the life of every true child of God. They are all indwelt by the Spirit of God, their lives are hid with Christ in God. 'At that day ye shall know that I am in my Father, and ye in me, and I in you' (John 14:20).

The other element—being subordinated to the Father and the Son in every word and action—is far from being realized in the life of every true believer. Yet this is to be their goal and pattern. And, to the extent that this is achieved, their lives too will exhibit that oneness with one another which can only be accounted for in terms of a common allegiance to an indwelling sovereign God who holds unhindered sway in their lives. It was for this that our Lord prayed.

The *means* which the Father will use to achieve this oneness in the lives of all His children—for He loves them equally—is the truth, His Word. To that end He has chosen to use His servants, that through them His people might be fed in due season, and thus be built up in the most holy faith. That is why the ascended Lord gave, and continues to give, gifts of ministry to His people (Eph. 4:2-16). And we would do well to remind ourselves constantly that what we are presented with in this passage in Ephesians is not a picture of a number of puny little bodies (or churches) isolated from each other, but one body, one people, who enjoy a common provision of ministry—the labours of those servants of God whose joint function it is to serve the body in the various capacities that are enumerated—that the entire body might benefit. 'Till we all come into the unity of the faith [doctrine], and of the knowledge of the Son of God [experience], unto a perfect man, unto the measure of the stature of the fulness of Christ [life and character]' (Eph. 4:13).

This is clearly God's will for His people, and in particular for those who, taken together, share the responsibility for their spiritual oversight and edification. Whatever might be our understanding of the permanence or otherwise of the various offices mentioned in the Ephesian passage (4:8-11), while they are not to be thought of as a separate hierarchical order they do represent an ongoing provision of ministry whose common aim and intention must be governed by that which is clearly laid down in Scripture—'Till we *all* come' (no one is to be abandoned or ignored if it is within our power to help them) to realize the tripartite oneness of doctrine, experience and character which is laid down in Scripture.

In other words, *truth matters supremely.* It is essential, not just for some vague concept of the intellectual well-being of the people of God, but in order to bring about in their lives their ever-increasing consecration to, and identification with, the sovereign will of God in all its parts. Furthermore, it must be truth held or spoken in love (Eph. 4:15), not because of any choice or preference on our part, but because we are under explicit instructions to love one another, as the Lord has loved us *all* (John 13:34; 1 John 2:9; 3:14; 4:7,21).

Governed as we are by these considerations, the Movement has rigorously resisted the temptation—attractive as it has been at times—to restrict its fellowship to individuals or churches who avow an allegiance to a truth (or truths) by virtue of which they can be distinguished from other evangelical Christians or fellowships of Christians. This must not be taken to mean that in our estimate truth is unimportant, or that deep-seated convictions with respect to such truths are matters of little consequence. We can say unequivocally that we are not interested in advocating unity at the expense of truth, or in behaving as though these differences did not exist or even matter. The very opposite is the case. It is precisely because we believe that the pursuit of truth in all its parts—doctrinal, spiritual and ethical—is so important, that we have advocated throughout the years a fellowship at church level which could conceivably embrace *all* evangelical churches. And we have done so in order that all the people of God, through their leaders, can engage honourably, and without causing embarrassment to anyone, in the pursuit of that truth to the mutual edification of the entire body.

To underline the importance we attach to this consideration, we would reiterate the principle which has guided us throughout the years. It is not because truth is unimportant, but because truth is *so* important, that we have refused to break fellowship with truly born-again believers who could be in error on certain matters of theological understanding. Just as most evangelical churches accept into membership those who have made a credible profession of faith, and do not demand, as a condition of fellowship, agreement with every item stated in their doctrinal standards (though they may require that they will not dissent from the proclamation of such standards), so we would maintain that, as a biblically warranted concession to the same imperfection of theological grasp, we should not refuse to be identified with other churches whose evangelical standards may not totally coincide with our own. The only qualifications we would make—and to these we shall return later—are, that within our own church fellowship we reserve the right to declare ourselves fully according to our own convictions, and that we should not be required to do anything in public which would be inconsistent with those convictions.

Indeed, we would wish to emphasize further the *positive* aspect of this scriptural principle. It would be our submission that those who maintain that they have a firmer and more accurate grasp of biblical truth are under an obligation to help those who are weaker in the faith (Rom. 15:1). This is why it is our hope and expectation that all ministers and church officers associated with our work will continue to give themselves to the task of helping each other, and helping as many as possible of God's children, as opportunity and occasion permit, to come to a fuller grasp of the truth of God. Because of the ever-present pressure (much of it carnal) to hive off with others of like mind to a 'denominational' or 'sectional' provision, the obligation to help each other into the truth is a need often not recognized or even acknowledged by Christians. Indeed, all too often it is shrugged off with a disdain which is altogether unworthy of those who profess to be followers of the One who said, 'Inasmuch as you have done it unto one of the least of these my brethren, you have done it unto me' (Matt. 25:40). Demanding as such a task may often be, it is surely better than to abandon each other to the error of our ways—a stance which, regrettably, is all too often adopted.

6
Coping with our differences

At this point we do need to address ourselves more carefully to the difficulty some churches feel at the prospect of being identified in any way with churches with whom they disagree on some article of doctrine or of church order. The classical answer to this problem in the past has been the 'denominational' approach. Churches of the same mind with respect to a particular doctrinal 'denominator' form themselves into a fellowship of churches which excludes churches not in agreement with them upon the doctrine (or doctrines) at issue. One justification for such a practice is that it serves as a public reproof of churches which in their judgment are in error. The inevitable consequence, however, in our day as in every other day, is that the doctrines which *some* hold in common are allowed to have more of a determining influence upon church relationships than the great body of doctrines upon which *all* would be agreed. And when this leads to the breaking of any meaningful links of fellowship with other evangelical churches, the body of Christ is rent asunder.

In our view there is another alternative. In the first place, we must all learn to respect the fact that local churches, through their leadership, cannot but assert themselves in terms of their conscientiously held doctrinal position. We must also accept the inevitable consequence that when such churches are known to hold divergent views on matters of doctrine, this will of necessity have a limiting effect on what they can be seen to be doing together in a local context. But this does not mean that they should disown each other totally! They are God's children. They own allegiance to the same Lord. One day they are destined to spend eternity together in His glorious presence. What is needed is that:

1. they acknowledge each other as churches which hold to the evangelical faith;
2. with respect to matters upon which evangelicals are divided, they insist on their obligation and duty to teach and to preach according to their lights;
3. as churches they accept each other's right not to be required to be formally associated with any function or activity that would in any way compromise or contradict their doctrinal position;
4. as opportunity is given, at the level of leadership particularly, they endeavour to do everything within their power, in a spirit of love and mutual respect, to help each other into the knowledge of the truth.

Association with the Movement and its activities would mean churches identifying themselves with this fourfold stance. It is our conviction that such an attitude of solicitous concern for each other—not at the expense of truth, but in the interest of truth—could only bear God's blessing.

There is one important rider which must be added at this point. It follows that such churches would themselves, in a spirit of love, exercise careful discipline within their own fellowship with respect to any teaching or practice thought to deviate from the plain teachings of the Scriptures. To fail to do so would be to make mockery of any public avowal of allegiance to the teachings of the Word of God. A commitment to exercise such discipline must therefore be required of all churches desirous of acknowledging publicly a relationship with each other through their mutual association with the Movement (see section (a)iv(g) in Appendix B).

Those who have been identified with the Movement in the past have endeavoured to encourage this attitude of loyalty to the Word of God, allied to a concern that *all* Christians may know the truth of God in all its fulness. It is a matter for rejoicing that the greater part of such a ministry is being undertaken by pastors and elders, men of God's appointment, teaching and preaching God's Word in the local churches where they have been placed. It is equally gratifying to note that the number of such men is increasing very considerably at the present time, as is also the volume of sound scholarly literature which will undergird their ministry.

More is required, however, than that which takes place within the confines of the local church, crucial and comprehensive as that provision is intended to be. At the level of leadership particularly, servants of God have for many years benefited through the opportunities afforded them for discussion, fellowship and prayer in the ministers' fellowships associated with the Movement and at the annual ministers' conferences (see Appendix C). In these and in various other ways ministers have been able to discuss matters which require careful deliberation, including subjects upon which Christians and their leaders in the past have been divided. They need to go on pursuing these things.

As has already been mentioned, in more recent years, with the emergence of new evangelical churches, church issues conferences were convened in North and South Wales, providing an opportunity for ministers and elders from different churches to meet to encourage each other and to discuss matters of common interest. To some of these functions the members of the churches would also be invited. At the present time these meetings are increasing in number and significance. The following quotation, taken from a letter of invitation introducing and commending such meetings, will serve to illustrate their purpose:

> These conferences are intended for those who are committed, if not in fact, at least in principle, to an emerging church situation. Some are already face to face with such situations, and are having to think through many matters that are vital to the ordering of their lives as churches. Others are awaiting a clear intimation of the way they are to take. Some have been led to take such steps in years past, and yet feel that they would benefit from a detailed study of such matters in the light of the Scriptures. All those who are involved in leadership in such situations are welcomed to these conferences.
>
> The intention is to provide a forum for consultation and conferring together in the light of Holy Scripture, and to do so in order to provide for one another in our several situations the maximum benefit from the pooling of our studies and the sharing of our convictions. In other words, it is not our intention to work towards preparing a blueprint for the churches, nor in the course of discussion to insist upon unanimity on all matters.

One reason why it was decided in 1967 that the Movement be affiliated to the British Evangelical Council was that by this means it (and the churches which it represents) could participate in similar consultation with church leaders from other parts of Britain.

Still more is needed, however, than that (1) we acknowledge each other's presence and tell the world that we are one; (2) we show, by the same token, that we are to be distinguished from apostate churches, and (3) we work towards realizing that unity of mind and purpose for which our Lord prayed. There are certain things which we can and ought to do for each other's benefit.

7
Serving one another

Throughout history church leaders have felt it right to act together in order to provide for the churches, and for the Lord's people generally, that which would otherwise be lacking. We believe that there is biblical warrant for this. *The ascended Lord gives to His church men who are gifts not only to the local church but to a regional and even a national situation* (Eph. 4:8-16). And such men have taken decisive action in the past. The convening of church councils in the early centuries, the provision of theological training, the ministry of itinerant preachers (conferring with and respecting the judgment of other church leaders), the production of Christian literature, are instances that immediately spring to mind.

In the New Testament itself, this attitude of caring for God's people generally is clearly illustrated in the life and teaching of the apostles and the other elders with whom they were associated. It was the apostles James, Cephas and John who, when they perceived the grace of God given to Paul and his companion Barnabas, extended to them 'the right hands of fellowship; that we should go unto the heathen, and they unto the circumcision' (Gal. 2:9). It was to the apostles that the church at Antioch resolved to send Paul and Barnabas, in order that they, with the concurrence of the elders and the whole church at Jerusalem, might advise how best to deal with the Judaizers (Acts 15:2). Indeed, the whole of the New Testament is a tribute to the depth and integrity of the concern felt by the apostles, and those who laboured with them, for the interests and spiritual well-being of God's people generally. It was the apostles who wrote the gospel narratives, or who helped and encouraged others to do so. It was they who wrote one epistle after another, to churches and individuals alike, warning against false teachers and exposing false doctrine. Time and again the apostle Paul would send men to help the churches, commending them warmly. At other times he would take men with him, that they might be fellow-labourers for the truth. Without question it was the quality of his pastoral concern that sustained the churches in their resolve to remember the poor at Jerusalem.

We do not dispute the fact that the apostles' office and function were altogether unique. Despite the protestations of Rome, none can be added to their number. They have no successors. Upon twelve thrones, and only twelve, they will sit to judge the quick and the dead. We do insist, however, that their sense of responsibility, ranging far beyond the confines of a local church, has stood as a challenge and inspiration to all who have followed in their *spiritual* lineage—men who have known a divine compulsion to take the gospel to the farthest reaches of the earth, and who have also known something of 'the care of all the churches' laid upon their hearts.

As in New Testament days, so it has happened subsequently. Men whom God had separated to the ministry of the Word have taken it upon themselves to provide what they felt needful for the benefit of God's people at large. Sometimes they have done this on their own; more often than not they have acted in concert with others. And throughout history, in the estimate of those whom they thus served, this was as it should be. The men whose gifts and calling others had tested were the ones to whom the people of God would look to provide what would help the churches generally. Churches and denominations which believed in the principles of episcopal or presbyterian church government had a ready-made hierarchical structure to hand which enabled them to recognize and to separate men to positions of leadership and special responsibility among their churches. Churches committed to the principle of independency (at least in pre-Union days) had no such provision. And yet, even amongst themselves they would be quick to recognize special gifts and callings, and would encourage others to undertake special tasks in the interest of all the churches (as witness the founding of the early nonconformist academies).

The same principle needs to be respected in our day. It is those who have been separated to the ministry of the Word in the churches, and *who share a burden for God's people generally*, who should be entrusted with ultimate responsibility for any wider provision for the churches. There should be no dichotomy at this point. Every effort should be made to ensure that all extra-church activities, whether at the local, regional or national level, should be seen as manifestations of the work of the churches. (They should never be allowed to become an embarrassment to them or, at worst, a threat to their well-being.) And the only way to make certain that this happens is by ensuring that those who are ultimately responsible are the men to whom God has entrusted the oversight of His people in the churches. This does not mean that they themselves would undertake all the tasks involved. As in the local church, so in the church of the Lord Jesus Christ at large, their responsibility would be 'to perfect the saints for the work of ministry' so that the appropriate 'joints of supply' are encouraged to function effectively and thus contribute towards the edifying of the entire body.

At this point we would like to explain how, up to the present at least, we have endeavoured to realize this biblical objective. Having done so, we will in the next chapter seek to answer the question that is often asked, 'Does this mean that the Movement is becoming another denomination?'

As already noted, since 1956 the Evangelical Movement of Wales has brought together gatherings of ministers to monthly fellowship meetings (and an annual ministers' conference[1]) for the purpose of study, discussion and prayer, and 'for the encouragement of such expressions of their oneness in Christ and of their obligation to serve Him together at the local level as they themselves would consider necessary, wise and practicable'. Since 1961 the Movement has also brought together regional committees which act in an executive capacity and endeavour to further within their own region the objectives, as outlined in this booklet, to which the Movement is committed. These committees consist of:

a) representatives of the ministers' fellowships. These would be ministers who feel a measure of responsibility for the wider work within their own region, and who, with the concurrence of their churches, would be prepared to devote some time to the consideration of those needs and how they should be met.

b) leaders of evangelical fellowships.

c) (since 1967) appointed delegates of affiliated churches. Wherever possible, the pastors of such churches would be expected to attend, together with such elders/deacons as have been appointed by the churches themselves (see Appendix B).

Regional committees appoint their own officials. As it is understood that their chairman will represent the work in that region on the Movement's General Committee, each regional committee would consider very carefully who among them had the wider work of God throughout the land sufficiently at heart to be prepared to undertake this further commitment. And it is those regional committee chairmen, together with

a) those who hold office under the Movement (annual conference secretaries, chairmen of the magazines' editorial boards, camps committee and finance committee, directors

[1] Since 1982 an annual Welsh ministers' conference has also been convened.

of the theological training and Christian study courses—each of them, in addition to their duties and obligations to the local church to which they belong, avowing an interest and a caring concern for the work of God throughout the land)

b) the Movement's trustees, eight in number

c) certain members of staff, and

d) others appointed by the General Committee to make its complement as representative as possible of the work of God generally in our land

—that form the Movement's General Committee. It in turn appoints two Executive Committees, one of which deals exclusively with matters relating to the Welsh-speaking population.

In this way, those who are in positions of leadership in the churches, *and who have a burden for the wider work of God in our land,* are able to meet at both regional and national level to give a lead with respect to the manifold obligations incumbent upon us as God's people acting together. They meet as servants of the churches, and not as representatives of a society existing apart from and independently of the churches. In their capacity as church leaders they determine the nature and scope of the work and witness undertaken either in the name of the Movement or, if it is considered more appropriate, in the name of the churches, both within their own region and further afield.

The following list will give some indication of the kind of services which, up to the present at least, have been considered prudent and needful in our day. It is a list which, needless to say, is subject to constant review and amendment:

(1) the planning of a programme of camps, annual conferences, residential conferences, etc., intended to serve the interests of churches, church members, and all who can be helped in their understanding of the Christian faith.

(2) the publication and distribution of Christian literature in both languages. This includes the work of the editorial boards of the *Evangelical Magazine of Wales* and *Y Cylchgrawn Efengylaidd;* the publishing programme of the Evangelical Press of Wales; the provision of Christian bookshops serving the interests of churches in different parts of Wales, various endeavours to disseminate Christian literature throughout our land through the support of workers in a full- or part-time capacity, visiting homes, fairs, schools, etc.

(3) the provision of conference centres for the use of the churches and of other evangelical agencies, as well as functions organized by the Movement.

(4) providing opportunity for evangelical ministers to meet for fellowship and conferring together.

(5) encouraging the formation of inter-church gatherings of church officers and (where necessary) co-ordinating their programmes.

(6) representing the convictions and beliefs of evangelical believers to secular authorities and to the media, and making representations on their behalf as required.

(7) the provision of theological training, counsel and advice for those called to the ministry of the Word.

(8) through the Christian Study Course, providing a guided course of study for individual Christians who are anxious to apply themselves to a systematic study of the Christian faith so as to be of greater usefulness in the local church.

(9) under the auspices of the Evangelical Libary of Wales, collecting and making available to churches and to individual Christians theological works and other evangelical literature, together with the publication of lectures etc. that reflect our rich spiritual heritage.

(10) through the EMW Trust Company Limited, offering to the churches schemes for church covenanting, as well as custody of church properties as sole or joint trustees (on the

clear understanding that such arrangements can be terminated by the churches).

(11) representing the churches in Wales on other bodies which serve the wider evangelical constituency in the UK, such as the British Evangelical Council and Go Teach Publications.

(12) through representation on the Association of Christian Teachers of Wales, the Christian Council for the Schools of Wales, etc., strengthening the links between such bodies and evangelical churches throughout the land.

All this must not be taken to mean that other church leaders may not take similar initiatives. They may well do so—indeed the situation may arise, as in the past, when they will need to do so. But inasmuch as an honest endeavour has been made to see that the provision developed over the past few years approximates as closely as possible, both in its spirit and intent, to the New Testament principles of love for each other in the truth, it is to be hoped that such initiatives will not be of a divisive nature, but rather that the possibility of embracing what is already provided and agreed (and so in every probability improving it) will at least be considered.

Neither does this mean that some local churches will not take certain initiatives of their own, e.g. in church planting and literature outreach work. The New Testament is full of instances of this kind. Indeed, it would be our conviction that this, together with the ministries of outstanding preachers whom God raises up from time to time, is the divinely prescribed way whereby the kingdom of God comes in strength and power in every day and age.

But churches are not intended to be isolated from each other. They were certainly not insular in their thinking in New Testament days. Letters which were sent to one were sent to all. They all acknowledged the same ministry. They all cared and prayed for each other. And what held them together was not a tight ecclesiastical structure, or the efforts of one or a few strong churches, but the ministry of men whom God had given as gifts to the churches in their day.

> It was these men, the fellowship that existed between them, their visits, their journeyings together, their writings, the things associated with their persons and calling, that constituted the only links of fellowship between congregations. This, and their proud belief and conviction that they all belonged together to one body by virtue of their faith in its Head and the fact that they were all vitally related to Him. In other words, what made them feel that they belonged together was not that they had entered as churches into a voluntary association with like-minded churches (which effectively excluded others); nor was it because they held in common certain truths that were not being upheld in the same way or as faithfully by other churches. They knew they belonged together because of these two facts: first, they belonged to the same body, and secondly, that one body was served by a company of men whom the Lord had given to the whole church. It is this that constitutes the entire New Testament perspective on evangelical unity—this, and nothing more.[1]

And it is these considerations, in essence, that we are seeking to respect in the work of the Evangelical Movement of Wales.

[1] Quoted from an address on the subject 'Facing Our Differences', given by the writer at the Annual Conference of the British Evangelical Council held at Leeds in 1976.

8
By what name?

At this point it has to be conceded that the term 'Movement', as used in our title 'The Evangelical Movement of Wales', does appear somewhat unfortunate. As Dr. Lloyd-Jones rightly pointed out during the latter years of his ministry, the last hundred years has witnessed a proliferation of 'movements', most if not all of them intended to make up for some deficiency in the life and witness of the churches, and all of them together helping to postpone the day when Christians would have the courage to consider again the doctrine of the church. Such movements, by and large, have functioned independently of the churches. At times they have even given the impression that the life and worship of a local church, encumbered with the care of the elderly, the lame and the poor, were for lesser mortals than themselves. Above all, however much lasting benefit they may have brought to God's people, many of these otherwise laudable 'movements' have unwittingly delayed the day when evangelicals would face up to the great challenge and need of our time—the reformation of the church of the Lord Jesus Christ according to the teachings of the Scriptures.

It is not in that sense that the term 'Movement' was first suggested or adopted as part of our title.[1] It is not in that sense either that it has been understood over the years. The Movement came into being when there were no churches to whom its work could be subordinated. For that reason, those who witnessed its growth and development in those years could be forgiven for thinking that it was a reforming movement in the more limited sense of that word. But even at that time, those who were involved in the leadership of the work, if only because they were themselves ministers and elders, were persons of deep conviction concerning (a) the place of the local church, and (b) the obligation laid upon us by Almighty God to subject all our thinking with respect to the ordering of the lives of His people to the teachings of the Scriptures.

As a consequence, any steps that would arrogate to the Movement duties or privileges that belonged to the local church were rigorously resisted. The suggestion made in the early years that Christians should become *members* of the Movement was firmly rejected: Christians were to be in membership in a local church. From the very earliest days, it was agreed that the Movement would not organize any meetings (other than young people's camps) that would take Christians away from their churches on the Lord's Day. Churches could do so if they so desired: the Movement would not. It was agreed also that all who served the Movement in any capacity would have to be in membership in a local church. The suggestion that the Movement should have an honorary president was ruled out altogether.

Perhaps the most significant feature, and the one which has served most of all to safeguard the work from growing away from the life of the churches (or being regarded as distinct from them), was that from the outset, as our Constitution clearly shows, every effort was made to see that those in

[1] It was at the suggestion of Dr. Lloyd-Jones at the Annual Welsh Conference held in Denbigh in 1955 that the title 'The Evangelical Movement of Wales' was adopted.

positions of leadership and responsibility in the churches (and particularly those amongst them upon whose hearts a care for the wider work of God had been placed) should also be ultimately responsible for the wider work of the Movement and all its activities.

It would be true to say that in one respect at least we are most grateful to God that we were led (as we now believe) to adopt this title. When it was decided in 1967 to make provision for churches to be affiliated to the Movement, the last thing that we desired was that the Movement and the churches formally associated with it should confine their fellowship and interest to such churches alone. That would be to deny all our convictions with respect to the oneness of the people of God and our obligation to work together towards realizing that oneness in doctrine, conduct and life which is to characterize them here on earth. Such an outcome would have been inevitable, however, if at that time in our history we had changed our title and called ourselves a fellowship of evangelical churches. Such a fellowship would of necessity have to exclude non-affiliated churches, and the effect—though unintended—would be yet further to divide the body of Christ.

That is why, whilst it is our desire that churches should affiliate with the Movement, it is *equally* our desire that they should only do so if they share our conviction that we belong—with others who may not be officially linked with us—to an ongoing movement of the Spirit of God in our day, and that it is our bounden duty, as a people, to endeavour to achieve that quality of fellowship and concern for all God's people which will resemble that which is so clearly portrayed in the pages of the New Testament.

That is also why, at all levels of our work and ministry, it has never been our intention—nor is it now—to confine our interest or our services to churches which are officially affiliated to the Movement. By virtue of their being affiliated, such churches will inevitably be more directly involved in organizing the Movement's work, but the work itself, at local, regional and national level, will always be concerned to serve a wider constituency.

Throughout the years it has been our policy to invite those in positions of leadership in the churches to serve on our committees, regardless of whether their churches were affiliated. For the same reason Christians in general are invited to our conferences, and to send their children to our camps. Our literature and the services of our bookshops, our theological training and Christian study courses, the use of our conference centres and all our other services, are intended for the benefit of *all* Christians and *all* churches faithful to the Word of God. *All* evangelical ministers are invited to our ministers' fellowships and conferences. All we ask is that they should respect the need to adhere as closely as possible to the teachings and demands of the Word of God, as they apply both to their own lives and to their churches (see Appendix C, section (a)).

At the local level, the ideal of fellowship would be to see evangelical churches in a given locality supporting each other's functions (provided that offence would not be taken if churches abstained from functions they found embarrassing) and making use of mutually helpful activities such as the Church Issues Conferences and similar spontaneous, locally based, occasional inter-church gatherings for officers or church members.

The apostle Paul did not hesitate to address his letters to 'the church' that met in Corinth, even though in every probability such a designation embraced a variety of congregations meeting in a plurality of spiritual homes, each powerfully affected by devious schismatic and polarizing influences. That is the biblical perspective, and that must be ours too—to aim for, at the very least.

Does this mean that the Movement is becoming 'another denomination'? We emphatically deny that this is the case for the following reasons.

In the first place, a denomination is a structured fellowship of churches having as a distinctive feature (marking them out and separating them from other churches) the upholding of a truth or truths which are not held by all Christians. The Movement has rigorously refused to adopt such a stance. Nor is it the intention now or at any other time, as already explained, to confine our interest, concern or facilities to churches affiliated to the Movement.

Secondly, when churches are affiliated to a denomination, it is they (and they alone) who are invited to attend assembly or synodical meetings, where matters which are the exclusive concern of those churches are discussed and agreed. The Movement has no such provision. Churches affiliated to the Movement are obviously free to gather together from time to time upon their own initiative in order to meet a spontaneous need, but this is in no way required of them. Affiliated churches remain totally autonomous. There is no provision within the Movement for their affairs to be discussed, or for anything to be prescribed for them in consequence of their affiliation.

When we think therefore of our title 'The Evangelical Movement of Wales', we have in mind nothing less than an aspect of the ongoing movement and activity of the Spirit of God in our land, and a serious intention to be as sensitive to that movement of the Spirit and as closely related to it as possible. Because it involves sinners who are called upon to 'perfect holiness in the fear of God', it will need to subject itself to constant reformation in the light of the Word of God. It will insist upon the primary role of the local church. At the same time it will call for the honouring of obligations which go beyond the brief or capacity of any one local church.

* * *

Since its inception the EMW has restricted its understanding of its function to the fulfilment of the objectives which we have outlined. It intends to continue doing so. But it is concerned that this should be done, and that it should be seen to be done, as a biblically warranted expression of the life of the churches, and not as something that belongs to the platform or programme of a Movement existing apart from the churches and therefore independent of them. This can only be achieved to the extent that churches (whether formally or informally) allow themselves to be identified with its objectives and involved in its work and witness.

Confronted as we are with the spectacle of churches and denominations which have long enthroned false doctrines coming together in the name of Christian unity, and even contemplating unity with a Church which, with all its false teachings, has insisted for centuries that it alone represents the body of Christ, let us not be found wanting in the grace and resolution that we shall need, both as individual Christians and as Christian churches, to honour those obligations to one another which are laid upon us in the Scriptures. 'For we are members of his body, of his flesh, and of his bones' (Eph. 5:30). May we be granted grace to acquit ourselves well, for His name's sake.

Churches desiring further information concerning affiliation, or clarification of any points raised in this booklet, are invited to write to the General Secretary, EMW, Bryntirion, Bridgend, Mid Glam. CF31 4DX.

APPENDIX A

DOCTRINAL BELIEF

(Clause 3 of EMW Constitution)

a) We accept the Holy Scriptures, as originally given, as the infallible Word of God, of divine inspiration. Recognizing them as our sole authority in all matters of faith and practice, we believe the doctrines taught therein. In particular we believe:

i) in the only true and living God, the Holy Trinity of Divine Persons in perfect unity, Father, Son and Holy Spirit, each of whom is co-equal and co-eternal, and sovereign in creation, providence and redemption.

ii) in the God and Father of our Lord Jesus Christ, who is holy, righteous, full of grace, mercy, compassion and love. In His infinite love He sent forth the Son, that the world through Him might be saved.

iii) in the Lord Jesus Christ, the incarnate Son of God, whose true humanity and full deity were mysteriously and really joined in the unity of His divine Person. We believe in His virgin birth, in His perfect life and teaching, in His substitutionary, atoning death on the cross, where He triumphed over Satan, sin and death, in His bodily resurrection and His ascension into heaven, where He now sits in glory at the right hand of God.

iv) in the Holy Spirit, the third Person of the Godhead, whose work is indispensable to regenerate the sinner, to lead him to repentance, to give him faith in Christ, to sanctify the believer in this present life and fit him to enjoy fellowship with God. For spiritual power and effectiveness His ministry is essential to the individual Christian and to the Church.

v) that as a result of the Fall all men are sinful by nature. Sin pollutes and controls them, infects every part of their being, renders them guilty in the sight of a holy God, and subject to the penalty which, in His wrath and condemnation, He has decreed against it.

vi) that through faith (and only faith) in the Lord Jesus Christ, whose death was a perfect oblation and satisfaction for our sins, the sinner is freely justified by God, who, instead of reckoning to us our sins, reckons Christ's righteousness to our account. Salvation is therefore by grace and not by human merit.

vii) that the Lord Jesus Christ will return personally, visibly and gloriously to this earth, to receive His saints to Himself and to be seen of all men. As the righteous Judge, He will divide all men into two, and only two, categories—the saved and the lost. Those whose faith is in Christ will be saved eternally, and will enter into the joy of their Lord, sharing with Him His inheritance in heaven. The unbelieving will be condemned by Him to hell, where eternally they will be punished for their sins under the righteous judgment of God.

b) All officers, committee members, speakers of the Movement, its fellowships and affiliated churches are required to subscribe to the above statement of belief.

APPENDIX B

CHURCHES

(Clause 4 of EMW Constitution)

a) Churches which are in full agreement with the following statements pertaining to the doctrine, membership, ministry, task and sacraments of the Christian Church may affiliate with the Movement. They agree:

i) **Doctrine:** That the Doctrinal Belief of the Movement (Clause 3) represents a minimal statement of scriptural truth which all Christian churches affiliated to the Movement are required to confess.

Whilst full understanding of these doctrines is not to be required of candidates for church membership, they must be clearly affirmed in the official standards of affiliated churches, to which all who teach therein or in their name must conform.

Affiliated churches may in their own official standards **add** to this statement, providing that such additions are not in any way inconsistent with the latter. They must not be associated with any Council of Churches whose doctrinal standards are sufficiently comprehensive as to allow within its fellowship those who believe doctrines which conflict with or in any way contradict the plain meaning of this statement.

ii) **Membership:** That as the Church belongs to the Triune God, whether it be on earth or in heaven, it is to consist of those and only those who, professing faith in Jesus Christ, the eternal Son of God, as Saviour, Lord and God, whose death in their place constitutes the only ground of their salvation, have forsaken their sin and now seek to live a life of holiness by the power of the Holy Spirit.

It is the duty of each church affiliated to the Movement to examine with charity all candidates for membership, so as to ensure as far as humanly possible that such persons have in fact experienced the new birth, which alone will enable them to make the above profession sincerely.

iii) **Government and Ministry:** That when God calls a church into being, by that act He pledges Himself to provide for it, and does so through the gifts of ministry.

Each congregation shall be autonomous, and shall determine its own form of government and ministry in the light of its understanding of the New Testament, making its own appointments on the basis of the divinely accredited 'gifts' that are appropriate to each office.

iv) **Task:** That the task of a local church is to glorify God and to exalt the Lord Jesus Christ, who is the Head of the Church which is His body. This it does by pursuing the following objectives:

(a) In worship, prayer and praise to adore Him, ever seeking to grow in the knowledge of Him, and in all matters to obey Him.

(b) To proclaim to the whole world the gospel of salvation through faith in Jesus Christ, the eternal Son of God.

(c) To build up its members in holiness and conformity to the will of God according to the Word of God.

(d) To give clear instruction to new converts, so that they will understand as soon as possible the meaning, importance and implications of the whole counsel of God.

(e) To administer the sacraments (or ordinances) of Baptism and the Lord's Supper as instituted by our Lord.

(f) To show, by deed as well as by word, the compassion of Christ, thus furthering the will of God in the world.

(g) To preserve itself from error by bringing all its teaching and practice under the judgment of Scripture, and thus be enabled to pass on to mankind the faith once delivered to the saints.

(h) To promote the fullest possible co-operation in fellowship and witness with all churches and fellowships who embrace the evangelical faith.

v) **Sacraments:** That the Lord Jesus Christ when He was on earth instituted two sacraments to be observed by His Church until His return in glory to the world, namely, Baptism and the Lord's Supper.

Whilst each congregation shall determine its own mode of baptism, and its significance in relation to membership of the local church, it is mutually agreed that:

(a) its observance never automatically conveys regenerative grace;

(b) its subjects shall be, as far as it is possible to ascertain, believers (in the case of believers' baptism), and the children of believers (in the case of infant baptism).

With respect to the Lord's Supper it is agreed that it is never to be considered a sacrifice for sin, nor is there ever any change in the substance of the bread and wine.

b) Churches which are associated with a doctrinally mixed denomination but which are nevertheless in full agreement with the above statements (Clause 4a) may be considered eligible for affiliation, provided that:

i) they give a solemn undertaking to work towards the reformation of the church according to biblical principles.

ii) they declare their intention in principle and practice to work towards a scriptural expression of church unity.

iii) if the church body with which they are connected is associated with any Council of Churches whose doctrinal standards are sufficiently comprehensive to allow within its fellowship those who believe doctrines which conflict with or in any way contradict the plain meaning of the Movement's Doctrinal Belief, they officially declare their dissent.

c) Affiliation

i) Applications for affiliation will be considered by the General Committee on being given 21 days' notice of the recommendation of the Regional Committee concerned, and shall be accepted by resolution passed by a three-fourths majority of those present and voting.

ii) Affiliated churches of up to fifty members will be represented on the Regional Committee by their minister/pastor and one other representative; churches of more than fifty members, by their minister/pastor and two other representatives. Such representatives will normally be elders or deacons.

iii) Churches affiliated to the Movement shall retain full financial responsibility for all local commitments, properties, etc., but as the Lord prospers them they shall be expected to support financially such work as they share with other churches and fellowships through the Movement (e.g., literature, camps, national and regional conferences, etc.).

APPENDIX C

MINISTERS' FELLOWSHIPS

(Clause 5 of EMW Constitution)

a) Basis. These shall consist of ministers:

i) who subscribe to the Doctrinal Belief of the Movement.

ii) who are concerned to exercise a God-centred evangelistic and pastoral ministry and to be involved in the reformation of the church according to biblical principles.

iii) who are dissatisfied with the doctrinally mixed denominational position and opposed to the Ecumenical Movement because of its comprehensivist ecclesiology, but who nevertheless avow an intention, in principle and practice, to seek a scriptural expression of church unity.

iv) who emphasize the need and promise of revival and seek to know and to follow the direction in which God is moving in our day.

Ministers who subscribe to the Doctrinal Belief of the Movement, but who cannot subscribe wholeheartedly to any other part of the above basis, may attend, provided that by such attendance the basis of the Fellowships is in no way called into question.

b) Aims. They shall meet regularly:

i) for the study of the Word of God, the doctrines of the Christian faith, and other subjects relating to the Christian ministry (as chosen and scheduled for study by the Ministers' Fellowships' Sub-Committee and as particular issues arise).

ii) for prayer and spiritual fellowship.

iii) for the encouragement of such expressions of their oneness in Christ and of their obligation to serve Him together at the local level as they themselves would consider necessary, wise and practicable.

c) Formation and Leadership. These shall be convened on a regional basis by the Ministers' Fellowships' Sub-Committee, who shall appoint the first Chairman and Secretary. Thereafter the Chairman and Secretary shall be appointed by the majority vote of the Fellowship to serve for a period of three years. All those holding office must subscribe to the Doctrinal Belief of the Movement and be in full sympathy with the aims of the Movement.

d) **Representation.** Each Fellowship shall appoint:

i) one representative to the Ministers' Fellowships' Sub-Committee.

ii) three representatives to the Regional Committee. Where there is more than one Ministers' Fellowship in a region, each Fellowship shall appoint two representatives to the Regional Committee.

In the event of a representative moving from the region represented by the Fellowship, an interim representative shall be appointed by the Fellowship to complete his term of office.